Antonia Ford practised as a solicitor for 15 years and was a Partner at DAC Beachcroft and Head of Fraud at Clyde & Co before transferring to the Bar. She is a specialist Personal Injury and Credit Hire practitioner.

She has extensive experience of RTA litigation, highway claims, employment liability, occupiers liability and product liability. She has advised Claimants, Defendants and Insurers on procedure and litigation tactics across all complexity of claims and tracks. She has also been able to use her knowledge of civil fraud to act for both Claimants and Defendants in cases where fundamental dishonesty has been alleged.

A Practical Guide to the Pre-Action RTA Claims Protocol for Personal Injury Lawyers

A Practical Guide to the Pre-Action RTA Claims Protocol for Personal Injury Lawyers

Antonia Ford
Barrister – Pump Court Chambers (Middle Temple)
Solicitor (Non Practicing)

Law Brief Publishing

Published 2020 by Law Brief Publishing, an imprint of Law Brief Publishing Ltd
30 The Parks
Minehead
Somerset
TA24 8BT

www.lawbriefpublishing.com

Paperback: 978-1-912687-61-9

PREFACE

The Pre-Action Protocol for Low Value Personal Injury Claims in Road Traffic Accidents (the RTA Protocol) was first introduced on 30 April 2010 and initially provided a streamlined process for personal injury claims arising from road traffic accidents between £1000 and £10,000.

It was introduced in response to rapidly increasing claim numbers and costs which were considered to be disproportionate to the value and complexity of the claims pursued.

Since its initial introduction the RTA Protocol has undergone a number of evolutions, most notably the vertical extension, following MoJ consultation, to claims up to a value of £25,000.

For personal injury litigators the Protocols (of which there are a number of specialist protocols relevant to different types of litigation) are all pervasive effecting their interactions with all parties, analysis of appropriate cases to pursue and ultimately the steps taken within the litigation. Despite their objective of simplifying litigation and increasing access to justice the Protocols expose users to a number of potholes which could adversely affect the outcome for their client and result in both cost and damages sanctions.

With future changes proposed, including the introduction of a Litigant in Person portal allowing unrepresented claimants to pursue their claims and tariff damages proposed by Civil Liabilities ACT 2018 it is essential that practitioners have an excellent grasp of the portal rules to ensure they provide an efficient and competent service.

The aim of this book is to provide a practical guide to the RTA Protocol which can be used by Practitioners, whether claimant or defendant, to perfect the service provided on pre-litigation claims. It is not intended to exhaustive textbook on all aspects of the RTA Protocol or avoid the need to consult the full Protocol text. It is designed to identify areas where contention could exist or has existed and consider the Courts approach to these areas.

The law stated in this book is believed to be correct up to the 31st December 2019.

The full text of the RTA Protocol can be found at: www.justice.gov.uk/courts/procedure-rules/civil/protocol/pre-action-protocol-for-low-value-personal-injury-claims-in-road-traffic-accidents-31-july-2013.

Antonia Ford
January 2020

CONTENTS

INTRODUCTION
AIMS OF THE PROTOCOL

Since their introduction in April 1999 the Civil Procedure Rules (CPR) have tried to simplify procedures, reduce costs and balance the competing desires of reducing litigation whilst maximising access to justice.

In his final report, *Access to Justice (Final Report), July 1996*, Lord Woolf advocated that any Civil Justice System should:

1. be just in the results it delivers;
2. be fair in the way it treats litigants;
3. offer appropriate procedures at a reasonable cost;
4. deal with cases with reasonable speed;
5. be understandable to those who use it;
6. be responsive to the needs of those who use it;
7. provide as much certainty as the nature of the particular case allows;
8. be effective, adequately resourced and organised.

He identified that the litigation system in place at the time of his review was too slow, expensive, adversarial and uncertain. Along with the sweeping changes to the procedural rules, immortalised in the CPR, the Woolf reforms also established an expectation of openness and co-operation between parties from the outset. Although initially intended to be limited to disclosure and expert evidence Lord Wolf's concept of pre-action cooperation expanded into specialist Protocols and laid the foundations for the establishment of the RTA Protocol in 2010.

The link between Lord Wolf's original review and the RTA Protocol is clear when considered against the aims set out in paragraph 3.1 of the RTA Protocol:

> *'The aim of this Protocol is to ensure that—*
>
> *(1) the defendant pays damages and costs using the process set out in the Protocol without the need for the claimant to start proceedings;*
>
> *(2) damages are paid within a reasonable time; and*
>
> *(3) the claimant's legal representative receives the fixed costs at each appropriate stage.'*

As with the overriding objective the aims of the RTA Protocol should infiltrate and inform all actions taken by parties in low value road traffic claims and will undoubtedly impact the Court's interpretation of the Protocol and the conduct of parties prior to the issue of proceedings.

CHAPTER ONE
STAGE 1

1. Suitability of the Portal

1.1. General Considerations

The RTA Protocol, as its full name suggests applies only to road traffic accidents which results in personal injury. Paragraph 4.1 states:

> *'This Protocol applies where—*
>
> *(1) a claim for damages arises from a road traffic accident where the CNF is submitted on or after 31st July 2013;*
>
> *(2) the claim includes damages in respect of personal injury;*
>
> *(3) the claimant values the claim at no more than the Protocol upper limit; and*
>
> *(4) if proceedings were started the small claims track would not be the normal track for that claim.'*

The accident must have occurred on a highway or other public place in England and Wales (paragraph 1.1 (16)) and the duty owed must arise from the use of a mechanically propelled vehicle intended for the use on a road (s. 185 Road Traffic Act 1988). This limitation is important given recent increases in claims involving cyclists in collision with pedestrians. Such claims would fall outside the scope of the RTA Protocol.

There are, however, other factors which determine whether the RTA Protocol is the appropriate method for intimating a claim. The RTA

Protocol does not have retrospective effect and as such applies only to accidents which occurred after 30 April 2010 (paragraph 1.2).

The RTA Protocol, pursuant to paragraph 4.5, also expressly excludes claims:

> *(1) in respect of a breach of duty owed to a road user by a person who is not a road user;*
>
> *(2) made to the MIB pursuant to the Untraced Drivers' Agreement 2003 or any subsequent or supplementary Untraced Drivers' Agreements;*
>
> *(3) where the claimant or defendant acts as personal representative of a deceased person;*
>
> *(4) where the claimant or defendant is a protected party as defined in rule 21.1(2);*
>
> *(5) where the claimant is bankrupt; or*
>
> *(6) where the defendant's vehicle is registered outside the United Kingdom.*

Although the RTA Protocol expressly exclude protected parties this clearly does not debar injured children/protected parties utilising the fast access to justice offered by the RTA Protocol. This is made clear by the inclusion of specific rules controlling costs and interim payments for child claimants. Paragraph 6.6 expressly allows a parent or guardian to sign a CNF on behalf of a child and provisions relating to need for and suitability of a litigation friend under CPR r.21 will apply to subsequent proceedings under Part 8.

The exclusion of non-UK registered vehicles is also important when considering the volume of European registered vehicles on UK roads. Interestingly, there is no specific prohibition on commencing claims via the RTA Protocol where two UK registered vehicles are involved in an accident outside the UK.

1.2. Claim Value

1.2.1. Upper Limit

Claims intimated via the RTA Protocol must have a value of no more than the upper limit as set out in paragraph 1.2:

> *1. The 'Protocol upper limit' is—*
>
> *(a) £25,000 where the accident occurred on or after 31 July 2013; or*
>
> *(b) £10,000 where the accident occurred on or after 30 April 2010 and before 31July 2013,*
>
> *on a full liability basis including pecuniary losses but excluding interest.*

This figure is calculated on a full liability basis and is based on the total for both general and special damages. The quantum figures utilised are assessed by the claimant's reasonable belief as to the claims value. It is, however, incumbent on the claimant to make an accurate assessment of the claims value or to notify the defendant as soon as their reasonable belief on value changes.

In *Lyle v Allianz Insurance Plc* (Liverpool CC 30 November 2017) the claim was commenced within the RTA Protocol and due to limitation Part 8 proceedings were issued and a stay applied. The value of the claim was initially believed to lie within the RTA Protocol limits but subsequently, whilst the stay was in place, it became clear that the value was significantly higher. The claimant, however, took no action to lift the stay or notify the defendant as to the increased value until the passage of 2 years. The claim was struck out and the claimant's appeal was refused by HHJ Pearce.

The value, however, excludes vehicle related losses pursuant to paragraph 4.4:

> *'A claim may include vehicle related damages but these are excluded for the purposes of valuing the claim under paragraph 4.1'*

It is notable that the RTA Protocol applies a wide approach to the interpretation of vehicle related damage when considering quantum and paragraph 1.2 (18) of the RTA Protocol provides the following:

> *'vehicle related damages' means damages for—*
>
> *(a) the pre-accident value of the vehicle;*
>
> *(b) vehicle repair;*
>
> *(c) vehicle insurance excess; and*
>
> *(d) vehicle hire.'*

This distinction potentially results in claims with significant value being dealt with via the RTA Protocol. Although there is often a correlation between the severity of the vehicle damage and the injury sustained, modern vehicles provide increasing levels of protection to their occupants and are designed to dissipate impact forces around the vehicle. Vehicle damage can often, therefore, overshadow an injury award. This issue is further exacerbated where a claimant hires a replacement vehicle on credit. Many credit hire practitioners would not be surprised to see claims for replacement vehicles totalling £30,000, £40,000 or over. Theoretically, as a consequence of paragraph 4.4, claims with a total value far in excess of the multi-track limit could proceed via the RTA Protocol to a 20 minute hearing in a block list before a District Judge.

Although Lord Justice Jackson, in the judgment of *Philip v Willis* [2006] EWCA Civ 401, confirmed that credit hire claims could and should be dealt with via the RTA Protocol, he eluded to the likely distinction with claims involving 'very high credit hire' which might be considered unsuitable for the portal due to complexity of law or fact. The fact that the portal is not intended to deal with high value cases is further supported by his judgment at paragraph 9:

> *'This modified procedure is designed to minimise the expenditure of further costs and in the process to deliver fairly rough justice. This is justified because the sums in issue are usually small, and it is not appropriate to hold a full blown trial'*

It is worth noting that complexity as a reason for not pursuing a claim via the portal is not considered until Stage 2 at paragraph 7.76. It is, therefore, arguable that complexity does not impede a claim being commenced via the RTA Protocol if it fits with the parameters set out at paragraph 4.1 of the RTA Protocol.

1.2.2. Lower Limit

Paragraph 4.1 (4) confirms that the RTA Protocol is not suitable for claims where, if proceedings were commenced, the normal track would be the Small Claim Track. As such, claims which fall within the parameters of CPR r.26.6 should be commenced as a small claim and not via the RTA Protocol. With reference to a personal injury claim, any injury likely to recover over £1000 would be suitable for the RTA Protocol. It is, therefore, fair to say that most cases involving injury would fall to be intimated via the RTA Protocol. It remains to be seen what changes will occur when the small claims limit is increased.

The fact that a claim is valued over £1000 is based on the claimant's reasonable belief at the point the claim is intimated as made clear in paragraph 5.9:

> *'Where the claimant reasonably believes that the claim is valued at between £1,000 and the Protocol upper limit, but it subsequently becomes apparent that the value of the claim is less than £1,000,*

> *the claimant is entitled to the Stage 1 and (where relevant) the Stage 2 fixed costs'*

This issue was explored in the first instance judgment of *Bromley v Hewson* (Medway County Court, 06 September 2012) where a child claimant received less than £1000 damages. The Court concluded that the case remained suitable for the RTA Protocol because it was not evident at the outset that the value was 'plainly' less than £1000. Portal costs were, therefore, awarded.

2. Limitation

The time limit for commencing personal injury claims is prescribed by s.11 (4) of the Limitation Act 1980 and requires claims to be commenced within 3 years from the date the cause of action accrues (i.e. the date of the road traffic accident) or less commonly in road traffic accidents from the date of knowledge of the injured person[1]. This limitation period applies to claims irrespective of compliance with the RTA Protocol and irrespective of the value of the claim intimated.

Where limitation is about to expire and the parties have not been able to complete Stage 1 and 2 of the RTA Protocol proceedings must be issued under CPR Part 8 to avoid being statute barred. It is then necessary to apply for a stay of proceedings so that the RTA Protocol procedure can be progressed (paragraph 5.7).

> *'Where compliance with this Protocol is not possible before the expiry of the limitation period the claimant may start proceedings and apply to the court for an order to stay (i.e. suspend) the proceedings while the parties take steps to follow this Protocol. Where proceedings are started in a case in which this paragraph applies*

1 Assuming an adult claimant who is alive at the time the 3 year limitation period expires.

> *the claimant should use the procedure set out under Part 8 in accordance with Practice Directions 8B (the Stage 3 Procedure)'*

This position is mirrored within CPR PD 8B para.16.1 which confirms:

> *'Where compliance with the relevant protocols is not possible before the expiry of a limitation period the claimant may start proceedings in accordance with paragraph 16.2'*

When issuing Part 8 proceedings in these circumstances the Claim Form must confirm, pursuant to CPR PD8 para.16.2, that

> *'(a) the claim is for damages; and*
>
> *(b) a stay of proceedings is sought in order to comply with the relevant Protocol.'*

Although, CPR PD8B para.16.3 confirms that a claimant must send to the defendant a copy of the Claim Form and the Court Order staying proceedings no time frames are prescribed by CPR Part 8. In the case of *David Grant v Dawn Meats* [2018] EWCA Civ 2212 the Court of Appeal considered the effect of a stay granted in a claim commenced within the Pre-Action Protocol for Low Value Employers and Public Liability) Claims (EL/PL Protocol) on a parties obligations under CPR PD8B para.16.2 and CPR r.7.

In this case, the claimant suffered personal injuries following an accident at work and despite liability being admitted at Stage 1 of the Protocol procedure settlement proved impossible. Part 8 proceedings were issued in June 2016 due to limitation concerns and a stay was requested and granted by the Court. Service of proceedings did not occur until well outside the usual service deadline under CPR r.7.5. The defendant applied for a declaration that service had not been effective. If successful the defendant's application would debar recovery of damages because compliance with CPR r.7.6(3), governing extensions for service of the Claim Form, would be impossible and any new proceedings would face both a limitation defence and the procedural hurdles imposed by s.33 of the Limitation Act 1980. The defendant's application was rejected by DDJ Davy at first instance and approved by HHJ Gore QC on appeal. The matter proceeded to the Court of Appeal and the Lord Justices provided useful guidance on the overreaching effect of a stay on proceedings. LJ Coulson, in the leading judgment, concluded that a stay had the effect of 'freezing' all aspects of the proceedings and that 'no steps in the action, by either side, are required or permitted during the period of the stay'.

This approach is supported by the glossary to the CPR which provides the following definition:

> *'A stay imposes a halt on proceedings, apart from taking any steps allowed by the Rules or the terms of the stay. Proceedings can be continued if a stay is lifted.'*

Although *David Grant v Dawn Meats* relates to a different specialist protocol, paragraph 5.7 of the EL/PL Protocol includes identical provisions on limitation to those contained within the RTA Protocol. The Judgment, therefore, arguably has universal application across both Protocols.

It is, therefore, clear that as long as proceedings are issued and a stay obtained prior to the expiry of limitation the defendant will accrue no defence under the Limitation Act 1980 and there will be no obligation to serve proceedings until the stay expires or is lifted by request.

Once the stay is lifted the procedural position reverts back to the moment when the stay was first imposed. The claimant's service obligations recommence and the service deadline is calculated against the time left from the time limits prescribed by CPR r.7.5

3. Claims Notification Form

3.1. Commencing a Claim

A claim is commenced by submitting a Claims Notification Form (CNF) to the defendant's Insurer, usually electronically via www.claimsportal.org.uk (the Portal) and a Defendant Only CNF to the defendant by first class post (paragraph 6.1).

An oddity of the RTA Protocol is that a defendant is ordinarily defined as '*the insurer of the person who is subject to the claim under this Protocol*'. Exceptions to this definition are, however, contained within paragraph 1.1 (10) which confirms that where the context dictates a defendant can be identified as:

(a) the person who is subject to the claim;

(b) the defendant's legal representative;

(c) the Motor Insurers' Bureau ('MIB'); or

(d) a person falling within the exceptions in section 144 of the Road Traffic Act 1988 (a "self-insurer").

Given the distinction made between the defendant's Insurer and the defendant in paragraph 6.1, it would appear that the RTA Protocol envisages that the Defendant Only CNF should be served on the tortfeasor. The only express exception to this requirement is contained in paragraph 6.1(2) where a Defendant Only CNF is not required if the defendant is self-insured.

No guidance is given within the RTA Protocol governing the address required to effect service of the Defendant Only CNF and what happens when the defendant's address is unknown.

CPR r.6 provides rules controlling service within litigation and draws a distinction between service of a Claim Form and other documentation. Only when considering service of a Claim Form does the CPR provide guidance on what steps are required when an appropriate address is unknown (CPR r.6.9). No similar provision exists within the CPR for the service of documents other than the Claim Form. This is primarily because a party to proceedings has a duty under CPR r.6.23 (1) to provide an address suitable for service.

The Pre-Action Protocol for Personal Injury Claims draws an association between the CNF and a Letter of Claim at paragraph 5.5:

> *'Where a claim no longer continues under either Low Value Protocol, the CNF completed by the claimant under the Protocols can be used as the Letter of Claim under the Protocol unless the defendant has notified the claimant that there is inadequate information in the CNF'*

Recent cases have sought to elevate the importance of the CNF to that of a document akin to a Claim Form but the Courts have stopped short of making that direct comparison. It is, therefore, unlikely that CPR r.6.9 applies to Defendant Only CNFs.

It is also difficult to see how the requirement to serve a Defendant Only CNF on the tortfeasor meshes with the direct right of action against an RTA Insurer pursuant to r.3 European Communities (Rights against Insurers) Regulations 2002. This inconsistency is further heightened by the fact that the Defendant's address is not a mandatory field on either the CNF or Defendant Only CNF.

In the broadest interpretation of 1.1(10) (a) the Insurer could be '*the person who is subject to the claim*' where a claimant is exercising their direct right of action. This would require the claimant to commence their claim by sending two almost identical CNFs to the insurer which would seem a somewhat redundant obligation.

The CNF contains both mandatory and voluntary information deemed necessary to allow a defendant to investigate the claim presented and make a determination on liability. Paragraph 6.3 requires all mandatory fields to be completed and establishes an expectation that the claimant will make reasonable attempts to complete the voluntary sections.

> *'All boxes in the CNF that are marked as mandatory must be completed before it is sent. The claimant must make a reasonable attempt to complete those boxes that are not marked as mandatory'*

A failure to complete mandatory information by the claimant allows the defendant to drop the claim from the Portal pursuant to paragraph 6.8 and exposes the claimant to cost risk pursuant to CPR r.45.24:

> *'where the defendant considers that inadequate mandatory information has been provided in the CNF, that shall be a valid reason for the defendant to decide that the claimant should no longer continue under this Protocol'*

When the RTA Protocol was first devised contention existed between insurers and claimant advocates regarding the nature and extent of the information considered voluntary. This primarily centred on the failure to make the name of the claims management company compulsory as many insurers had concerns with the link between claims farming and fraudulent claims.

As a direct response to these fraud concerns the RTA Protocol was amended and access granted to claimant to the Claims Underwriting Exchange (CUE) via a web based portal called www.askCUE.co.uk. This database, populated by most insurers, provides details of previous personal injury claims registered with the DWP for a CRU certificate. Although Insurers have had unilateral access for many years, the move to grant access to claimant representatives was designed to assist in the completion of informed risk assessment by claimant solicitors before claims are intimated.

The requirement to interrogate CUE is compulsory pursuant to paragraph 6.3A (1). Where a CNF is submitted which does not include the necessary reference number the defendant can request a corrected CNF (paragraph 6.3A (2)) or can agree to dispense with re-service (paragraph 6.3A(3)). Where re-service is required the timeframes under the RTA Protocol do not commence until the corrected CNF is re-served.

3.2. Status of a CNF

The status of a CNF is not defined within the RTA Protocol. Where a claim falls from the Portal, the CNF takes the place of the Letter of Claim (paragraph 6.27). Paragraph 5.7 of the Pre-Action Protocol for Personal Injury Claims (PI Protocol) confirms:

> *'Letter of Claim and Response are not intended to have the same formal status as a statement of case in proceedings. It would not be consistent with the spirit of the Protocol for a party to 'take a point' on this in the proceedings, provided that there was no obvious intention by the parties who changed their position to mislead the other party'*

There are, however, marked differences between the two documents. A claim within the RTA Protocol could conceivably be intimated and settled with the CNF being the only formal document provided to the defendant.

In *Richards & Anor v Morris* [2018] EWHC 1289 (QB), Mr Justice Martin Spencer, introduced his judgment with the following observation:

> *'CNFs are important documents because not only are they the first notification of a claim to the potential defendant's insurer in low value personal injury claims in road traffic accidents where the damages sought are between £1,000 - £25,000 but also they will often be the basis for early settlement of the claim'*

Importantly a CNF is also supported by a statement of truth either signed the claimant's representative:

> *'The claimant believes that the facts stated in this claim form are true. I am duly authorised by the claimant to sign this statement.'*

Or the claimant:

> *'I am the claimant. I believe that the facts stated in this claim form are true.'*

This wording is identical to the prescribed wording for statements of truth in CPR PD.22 2.1 and 2.2.

A false statement on a document verified by a statement of truth without an honest belief in its truth exposes the signatory to the risk that Contempt of Court proceedings could be brought pursuant to CPR r.32.14 (1).

> *'Proceedings for contempt of court may be brought against a person if he makes, or causes to be made, a false statement in a document verified by a statement of truth without an honest belief in its truth.'*

This obligation is imposed irrespective of whether the statement of truth is signed by the claimant or his legal representative (CPR PD22 para. 3.8(3)). A CNF is not a category of document expressly identified in the CPR PD22 as requiring validation by a statement of truth. CPR PD22 para.1.1 is arguably not an exhaustive list it does not automatically follow that CPR r.32.14 would not apply to documents created under the RTA Protocol due to their absence from the list.

In *Liverpool Victoria Insurance Company Limited v Yavuz and Others* [2017] EWHC 3088 (QB) the High Court flirted with the potential for contempt proceedings stemming from a false CNF. The case related to an application for order of contempt made by Liverpool Victoria Insurance against 9 claimants accused of being part of a 'crash for cash' conspiracy. In his obiter comments Mr Justice Warby stated:

> *'It may be arguable therefore that a false and dishonest statement in a CNF in Form RTA1 could found an application to commit for contempt, but it cannot be said that the matter is free from doubt. To say that the court "will expect" compliance with a PAP is not necessarily equivalent to saying that parties must comply. The General PAP states that parties who do not comply may be asked for an explanation, and warns of costs consequences, but not of the prospect of contempt proceedings'*

In *Richards & Anor v Morris*, Mr Justice Martin Spencer took a stricter view that the CNF did provide the basis for possible proceedings for contempt of court.

In *Molodi v Cambridge Vibration Maintenance Services* [2018] EWHC 1288 (QB) inconsistencies between the CNFs and the claimant's witness evidence led to a finding of fundamental dishonesty and dismissal of the claim. Inaccuracies in the information contained within the CNF relating to the claimant's injuries, vehicle damage, occupants and rehabilitation needs were instrumental in the judgment and dismissal. Although potentially an extreme example of the potential problems with a CNF, the judgment arguably elevates the CNF to a level comparable with a Claim Form and has seen favour amongst District Judges considering cases in lower courts.

What is clear, therefore, is that a defendant and the Court is entitled to rely on the contents of the CNF as being true and that mistakes within the CNF expose the claimant to allegations of fundamental dishonesty and contempt.

4. Rehabilitation

The RTA Protocol requires confirmation of a claimant's rehabilitation needs within the CNF and advocates adherence to the Rehabilitation Code. Section C of the CNF requires a claimant to confirm both whether treatment has been recommended already by a medical professional and whether the claimant is aware of any other rehabilitation needs. Often, a CNF is produced before the finalisation of medicolegal evidence and as such the CNF requires a claimant to make an informed prediction of his needs. It is notable that the Rehabilitation Code places the duty to make that initial assessment of the claimant's need on the claimant's solicitor. It does, however, also place an expectation on the compensator that they will consider the claimant's rehabilitation needs throughout the life of the claim.

When considering offers of rehabilitation the claimant should weigh their options carefully and must act reasonably. Ordinary rules of mitigation apply to damage claims within the RTA Protocol, as such the burden rests on the defendant to prove that there has been a failure to mitigate:

'it is settled law that the onus of proving that a claimant failed to mitigate his damage lies on the defendant to show that the claimant ought, on the facts, reasonably to have pursued some course of action which he did not in order to mitigate his loss' Samuels v Benning [2002] EWCA Civ 858.

A Courts assessment of whether a claimant has acted unreasonably and failed to mitigate their loss is a matter of fact and, therefore, beholden to the discretion of the Judge. Both parties need to be aware of the balance of risk in assessing mitigation when considering offers of rehabilitation.

5. Defence Response

The RTA Protocol imposes two initial responsibilities on the defendant:

Paragraph 6.10 – '*The defendant must send to the claimant an electronic acknowledgment the next day after receipt of the CNF.*

Paragraph 6.11 – *The defendant must complete the 'Insurer Response' section of the CNF ("the CNF response") and send it to the claimant within 15 days'*

In reacting to the CNF a defendant has 6 potential responses, they can:

1. admit liability;
2. deny liability;
3. make an allegation of contributory negligence (other than related to seat belts);
4. fail to respond;

5. notify the claimant that the value falls below the small claims limit; or

6. allege that there has been a failure to complete mandatory information on the CNF.

Unless a defendant, within 15 days of receiving a CNF, admits liability (and any allegation of contributory negligence is limited to a failure to wear a seat belt) the claim will automatically exit the portal (paragraph 6.15).

A failure to electronically acknowledge a CNF does not cause the claim to automatically exit the RTA Protocol despite the mandatory character of paragraph 6.10. This interpretation is supported by Mr Recorder Morgan's judgment in *Jaykishan Patel v Fortis Insurance Ltd* (Leicester County Court 23 December 2011) where a claimant's decision to withdraw a claim from the RTA Protocol when a defendant failed to submit an acknowledgment was considered unreasonable.

Where a claim exits the RTA Protocol automatically at Stage 1 the claim falls to be governed by the PI Protocol pursuant to paragraph 6.17:

> *'Where paragraph 6.15 applies the claim will proceed under the Pre-Action Protocol for Personal Injury Claims starting at paragraph 6.3 of that Protocol (which allows a maximum of 3 months for the defendant to investigate the claim) expect where paragraph 6.15(4)(a) applies the claims will proceed under paragraph 5.1 of that Protocol.'*

As such unless the defendant has alleged that insufficient information is contained within the CNF this document will be viewed as the Letter of Claim and the defendant will have 3 months to investigate and respond on liability.

Where liability is denied the defendant must provide a brief explanation of their decision with their response (paragraph 6.16). Again there is no express sanction against providing a bear denial and, given that a defendant automatically has a further 3 months to provide a liability response once the matter exits the RTA Protocol, a failure to explain a liability decision is unlikely to be determinative in any conduct considerations by the Court.

CHAPTER TWO
STAGE 2

1. Progressing to Stage 2

A claim will proceed into Stage 2 when the claimant uploads a Stage 2 Settlement Pack to the Portal. Paragraph 7.32 anticipates that the claimant's evidence will be complete at the point of upload, although a stay can be agreed pursuant to paragraph 7.12 where extra medical or non-medical evidence is required.

'The Stage 2 Settlement Pack must comprise—

> *(1) the Stage 2 Settlement Pack Form;*
>
> *(2) a medical report or reports;*
>
> *(3) evidence of pecuniary losses;*
>
> *(4) evidence of disbursements (for example the cost of any medical report);*
>
> *(4A) in a soft tissue injury claim, the invoice for the cost of obtaining the fixed cost medical report and any invoice for the cost of obtaining medical records;*
>
> *(5) any non-medical expert report;*
>
> *(6) any medical records/photographs served with medical reports; and*
>
> *(7) any witness statements.*

Although the evidential burden, as with any litigation, remains with the claimant it is important to remember that the RTA Protocol is designed to be a streamlined and simplified process. His Honour Judge Parker in his judgement in *Fitton v Ageas* (Liverpool County Court 8 November 2018) provided the following description which is echoed in many judgments relating to the RTA Protocol:

> *'In my judgment the protocol for low value personal injury claims in road traffic accidents was introduced to streamline and simplify these sorts of claims of low value. It provides a self-contained code to enable parties to negotiate a settlement of sums for damages of such low value in these cases.*

The process has the potential to deliver what might be called fairly rough justice on occasion, but generally is a proportionate and cost-effective way to achieve settlement.'

There is, therefore, a clear expectation that the evidence required to support a claim will be limited. This view is consistent with the RTA Protocol which envisages that in most cases several categories of evidence will not be required:

Paragraph 7.5 – medical records - *'most claims with a value of no more than £10,000, it is expected that the medical expert will not need to see any medical records'*

Paragraph 7.9(1) – non-medical experts - *'In most cases, a report from a non-medical expert will not be required, but a report may be obtained where it is reasonably required to value a claim.'*

Paragraph 7.11 – witness statements - *'In most cases, witness statements, whether from the claimant or otherwise, will not be required. One or more statements may, however, be provided where reasonably required to value the claim'*

2. Status of the Settlement Pack

The Settlement Pack, as with the CNF, requires the claimant to validate its contents with a statement of truth. The wording is identical to the prescribed wording for statements of truth in CPR PD22 para. 2.1 and 2.2.

The document requires the claimant to set out the extent of the claim and the heads of loss being sought. It further allows the claimant to both comment on and evidence the quantum amounts being claimed. Against this back drop a defendant is encouraged to negotiate.

Although the status of the Settlement Pack was not expressly considered in *Richards & Anor v Morris*, the inclusion of a statement of truth on a CNF was a defining issue in Mr Justice Spencer's decision to place reliance on the content of a CNF when assessing a claimant's credibility under cross examination.

> *'the statement of truth is thus important as it means, or should mean, that the insurer can rely on the accuracy of the contents of the CNF in assessing the damages and any offer of compensation to be made'*

The two first instant decisions of *Smikle v Global Logistics* (Walsall County Court, 3 June 2016) and *Reardon v Mango Engineering Services Ltd* (Peterborough County Court 27 June 2018) explore whether reliance on the content of Settlement Packs is appropriate. Although not binding, when they are read alongside the judgement of LJ Spencer in *Richards & Anor v Morris* they become increasingly persuasive.

In both cases personal injury claims were commenced and settled within the RTA Protocol but subsequent proceedings for vehicle damage were pursued. In *Smikle v Global Logistics* the claimant failed to mention the existence of a credit hire claim within either the CNF or Settlement Pack and in *Reardon v Mango Engineering Services Ltd* a potential claim for vehicle repairs was mentioned in the CNF but was not subsequently pleaded in the Settlement Pack. The reliance to be placed on the Settlement Pack was considered in both claims.

In *Smikle v Global Logistics*, District Judge McQueen, in concluding that the second proceedings were an abuse

> *'I take the view that that signature on a Statement of Truth is holding out that that is what the evidence is, that is what the case is all about. In my view, the defendant is entitled to rely on that because otherwise they could face a potentially significant clam and it seems to me that in this case if it had only been highlighted under the appropriate section that vehicle hire was to be claimed I am sure the defendant's then insurer, having been put on notice, would have taken a very different view towards the conduct of proceedings. They would clearly have been on notice that there was a claim for hire, in this case a significant claim for hire, and it seems to me that they were entitled to place reliance on a certificate signed by a solicitor indicating that there was no claims for hire, and it seems to me if I of behind that then I am going behind now the whole spirit of the CPR and the rules that are now in place in that a signed Statement of Truth is deemed to be the statement on the part of the client made by his solicitor and that the document provided is and is a genuine reflection of the truth of the situation'*

It is understood that this issue has been considered by the Court of Appeal in the case of *Hillier v Southern Rock* (Newcastle County Court, December 2019). Access to the full judgment is currently not available but a finding that subsequent proceedings were an abuse was upheld.

3. Timing

The progress of a claim through the RTA Protocol is under the control of the claimant. The timing for commencing Stage 2 is governed by paragraph 7.33:

> *'The claimant should send the Stage 2 Settlement Pack to the defendant within 15 days of the claimant approving —*
>
> *(1) the final medical report and agreeing to rely on the prognosis in that report; or*
>
> *(2) any non-medical expert report,*
>
> *whichever is later'*

The reliance on the final medical report as the marker for commencement of Stage 2 introduces the risk for significant delay in the claims process. There is, for example, no guidance on when a medical expert should be instructed or what happens if a claimant or their legal representative delays in authorising the report once received. Similarly, there is no express sanction for failing to progress a claim into Stage 2 even where a finalised report has been received and authorised.

Lyle v Allianz Insurance Plc (Chester County Court, 21 December 2017) potentially, however, strikes a cautionary note to claimants who fail to progress claims within a reasonable time frame. Although primarily related to a failure by the claimant to monitor the value of their claim, the significant delay in progressing the claim was instrumental in the strike out of the claim. HHJ Pearce stated:

> *'in my judgment the claimant's significant and persistent failures and the consequent delay, increased expense and prejudice to the*

> *Defendant, amply justified the District Judge's refusal to lift the stay and his consequent order striking out the claim'*

Importantly, however, proceedings had already been issued due to limitation when the critical delays occurred albeit that the claim remained within Stage 2. As such the provisions of CPR r.3.4 relating to abuse of process were applicable. There is no similar mechanism to stifle a claim whilst it remains unissued within Stage 2 given its pre-litigation status and a parties rights under the Limitation Act 1980. It is, however, important for parties to understand how actions, or lack thereof, can have potential implications on the future stages of a claim. Unreasonable delay in commencing Stage 2 which ultimately result in the need to issue and stay proceedings could result in sanctions being applied by the court where sufficient prejudice can be shown to the defendant.

It is also unclear how the Court will view a claimant's failure to request a stay pursuant to paragraph 7.12 or a defendant's unreasonable refusal to allow extra time to finalise the medical or non-medical expert evidence.

4. Medical evidence

4.1. General Rules

Paragraphs 7.1 to 7.8A provides rules and guidance for the reliance on medical reports.

It is envisaged that most claims will require only one medical report but extra reports from other medical disciplines are allowed *'where the injuries require reports from more than one medical discipline'* (paragraph 7.2). It is expected that where a report is deemed unnecessary or unjustified a claimant will be unable to recover the disbursement when costs are considered although no case law, reported or otherwise, could be identified to assess the risks of none recovery in these circumstances.

A similarly cautious approach should also be taken to addendum reports or claimants will inevitably face successful cost arguments from defendants. Paragraph 7.8 confirms that any subsequent report from an existing expert must be justified and confirms that:

> *'A report may be justified where—*
>
> *(1) the first medical report recommends that further time is required before a prognosis of the claimant's injuries can be determined; or*
>
> *(2) the claimant is receiving continuing treatment; or*
>
> *(3) the claimant has not recovered as expected in the original prognosis'*

It is notable, however, that CPR r.45.19 (2) does not, unlike the counterpart provision for soft tissue injuries at CPR r.45.19 (2A), expressly maintain the requirement that a report needs to be justified for recovery of the disbursement. The rule instead favours the more general requirement that recovery is allowed for experts reports '*as provided for in the relevant protocols*'.

It remains to be seen whether the Courts will take a restrictive view of subsequent medical reports as has been taken in respect to other disbursements in Protocol or ex-Protocol claims.

Importantly, no fee is recoverable, except in exceptional circumstances, where the expert or an associate, has provided medical treatment to the claimant (or will provide such treatment as a result of the content of their report). CPR r.45.19 2B was clearly introduced to avoid unnecessary treatment being recommended and undertaken where there is a financial incentive on the expert for their recommendation. It, however, clearly has an impact on the recoverability of disbursements regularly seen within RTA Protocol claims. In particular, the discharge report claimed on many physiotherapy invoices should fall foul of this rule. They are, by their very nature, medicolegal reports and not necessary for the claimant's treatment. This is evidenced by the fact they usually attract VAT. Given that treatment will almost certainly have been provided by the author or an associate of the author the fee should not be awarded pursuant to CPR r.45.19 2B.

4.2. Soft Tissue Injuries

Paragraph 7.8A was added to the RTA Protocol as part of the significant civil rule changes introduced on 6 April 2015. These changes established an independent organisation (MedCo) with the remit of facilitating the instruction of medicolegal experts in soft tissue claims. The move was a reaction to a perception that medicolegal reports were not independent and were open to manipulation, bias and fraud when financial links existed between solicitors, medical agencies and medical experts.

Although often referred to as 'Whiplash Reforms Part 1', this is a misnomer and fails to accurately reflect the scope of their application to motor accident personal injury claims beyond neck and back injuries. Paragraph 1.1 (16A) defines a soft tissue injury claim as *'a claim brought by an occupant of a motor vehicle where the significant physical injury is a soft tissue injury and includes claims where there is a minor psychological injury secondary to the physical injury'*

There is no mention of the area of the body effected or the mechanism of injury save for the involvement of a motor vehicle within this definition. Similarly, there is no express definition for a 'soft tissue injury' within the RTA Protocol. It is notable that the ordinary dictionary definition of a soft tissue injury is simply a 'trauma or overuse of muscles, tendons and/or ligaments' and that the NHS limits 'whiplash' to pain and spasms in the neck and shoulders.

The application of the rules governing medical experts for soft tissue injuries is therefore, on the face of the RTA Protocol, wider than traditional 'whiplash' injuries usually associated with road traffic accidents.

The use of the phrase 'soft tissue injury' and the lack of clear definition may change when (and if) the Civil Liabilities Act 2018 gains royal assent. In this Act, introducing tariffed damages for certain injuries, the phrase 'whiplash injury' is immortalised and defined within section 1 of that Act as follows:

> *'Whiplash injury etc*
>
> *(1) In this Part "whiplash injury" means an injury of soft tissue in the neck, back or shoulder that is of a description falling within subsection (2), but not including an injury excepted by subsection (3).*
>
> *(2) An injury falls within this subsection if it is—*
>
> *(a) a sprain, strain, tear, rupture or lesser damage of a muscle, tendon or ligament in the neck, back or shoulder, or*
>
> *(b) an injury of soft tissue associated with a muscle, tendon or ligament in the neck, back or shoulder.'*
>
> *(3) An injury is excepted by this subsection if—*
>
> *(a) it is an injury of soft tissue which is a part of or connected to another injury, and*

(b) the other injury is not an injury of soft tissue in the neck, back or shoulder of a description falling within subsection (2).'

In keeping with the desire for independence paragraph 7.8B (1) confirms that '*the first report must be a fixed cost medical report from an accredited medical expert selected for the claim via the MedCo portal*'. This is designed to ensure that at least one report is produced using a random and fair selection process.

It is also important to note that the accredited medical expert need not be a General Practitioner. Paragraph 1.1 (12) defines a medical expert as

'a person who is—

(a) registered with the General Medical Council;

(b) registered with the General Dental Council; or

(c) a Psychologist or Physiotherapist registered with the Health Care Professions Council.'

Whilst it is difficult to see that a dentist or psychologist would be matched by MedCo to report on a whiplash type injury there is nothing which would preclude a suitably qualified and accredited physiotherapist from providing a report.

The need for extra medical reports is more closely controlled, by paragraph 7.8B, than in cases involving non soft tissue injuries and such reports, whether an addendum report or a report within a new discipline will only be considered justified where it has been recommended by the first expert and that initial report has been disclosed to the defendant.

Paragraph 7.8B (3) also places limits on the type of expert allowed for further medicolegal reports for soft tissue injuries:

> *'where the claimant obtains more than one medical report, the first report must be a fixed cost medical report from an accredited medical expert selected via the MedCo Portal and any further report from an expert in any of the following disciplines must also be a fixed cost medical report—*
>
> *(a) Consultant Orthopaedic Surgeon;*
>
> *(b) Consultant in Accident and Emergency Medicine;*
>
> *(c) General Practitioner registered with the General Medical Council;*
>
> *(d) Physiotherapist registered with the Health and Care Professions Council.'*

It is, therefore, a clear breach of the rules to obtain a report outside the MedCo Portal, commission an unjustified medical report or rely on further medical evidence when the first report has not been disclosed to the defendant. There is, however, no automatic sanction attached to non-compliance by a claimant of the rules relating to medicolegal reports and defendants should exercise caution in dropping cases from the RTA Protocol for non-compliance of arguably 'lesser' procedural rules. A claimant that fails to comply with the rules relating to medical evidence should be aware, however, that a defendant may choose to remove the case from the portal, argue that the claimant should be debarred from relying on the non-compliant medical evidence and/or that they should not be entitled to recover the costs of an unjustified medical report pursuant to CPR r.45.19 2A (b).

4.3. Status of the Medical Report

Importantly the rules confirm that after Stage 2 a claimant will not have the opportunity to amend or otherwise correct the reports once they are uploaded (paragraph 7.3),

> *'The claimant must check the factual accuracy of any medical report before it is sent to the defendant. There will be no further opportunity for the claimant to challenge the factual accuracy of a medical report after t has been sent to the defendant'*

This rule, when read with the judgments in *Richards & Anor v Morris* and *Molodi v Cambridge Vibration Maintenance Services,* increases the pressure on claimants to ensure that all evidence relied upon is accurate. Service of inaccurate evidence will expose them to a risk of a finding of dishonesty and/or cost sanctions should a defendant choose to drop the claim from the Portal and take a stand on the validity of the case being pursued.

5. Legal Advice

Given the inherent simplicity of claims within the RTA Protocol it is expected that the claimant's primary legal advisor will be able to value the claim. The RTA Protocol, however, envisages that advice may be justified (paragraph 7.10):

> *'In most cases under the Protocol, it is expected that the claimant's legal representative will be able to value the claim. In some cases with a value of more than £10,000 (excluding vehicle related damages), an additional advice from a specialist solicitor or from counsel may be justified where it is reasonably required to value the claim.'*

Other than value no guidance is given to assist in assessing whether specialist advice is justified or reasonable. It is important to note that recovery of the costs incurred in obtaining specialist advice is not guaranteed. Pursuant to paragraph 7.31(1) a defendant may refuse payment at Stage 2 and the Court may, at Stage 3, refuse to allow recovery where it is considered that the instruction was not reasonably required. The RTA Protocol, therefore, advises the parties to explain their decision regarding specialist legal advice (and additional medical evidence) within the Stage 2 process (paragraph 7.31(2)):

> *'Therefore, where the claimant obtains more than one expert report or obtains an advice from a specialist solicitor or counsel—*
>
> *(a) the claimant should explain in the Stage 2 Settlement Pack why they obtained a further report or such advice; and*
>
> *(b) if relevant, the defendant should in the Stage 2 Settlement Pack identify the report or reports or advice for which they will not pay and explain why they will not pay for that report or reports or advice.'*

Although not a mandatory requirement, the provision of a full explanation by a claimant to explain the decision behind instructing Counsel or by the defendant to explain their refusal to pay may avoid a dispute developing between the parties and may assist the Court in assessing the recoverability of the disbursement claimed.

6. Contributory Negligence

If a defendant alleges contributory negligence the claim automatically falls from the RTA Protocol unless the allegation relates to the failure by a claimant to wear a seat belt. Where a defendant alleges that a failure to wear a seat belt contributed to the claimant's injuries the claimant must comply with two rules at Stage 2:

Paragraph 7.34 – which requires the claimant to suggest a percentage reduction in damages as a consequence of this alleged failure (the percentage suggested may be zero) ; and

Paragraph 7.7 – which requires the claimant's accredited medical expert to provide sufficient information to enable the defendant to calculate the appropriate reduction of damages in accordance with the principles set out in existing case law.

7. Interim Payments

A claimant (except a child claimant) may request an interim payment of £1000 or more. A request for an interim payment, is made by submitting an Interim Settlement Pack to the defendant and must include the available medical evidence, confirmation whether further medical evidence is recommended and justified (paragraph 7.14) and evidence to support pecuniary losses and disbursements (paragraph 7.15).

Where the claim is worth over £10,000 a claimant may make more than one request for an interim payment (paragraph 7.21).

If the request is limited to £1000 the defendant must make payment within 10 days. Where the claimant requests a higher figure the defendant, within 15 days, has three options:

1. pay the full amount requested less any recoverable benefits;
2. make the minimum payment of £1000; or
3. pay another amount between £1000 and the total amount requested

Where the defendant chooses not to pay the full amount requested a brief explanation must be provide to explain their decision.

Where an interim payment is not made or not made for the amount requested the claimant can choose to remove the claim from the portal and issue Part 7 proceedings pursuant to paragraph 7.28. There is, however, pursuant to paragraph 7.29, an inherent cost risk in taking such action

'Where the defendant does comply with paragraph 7.19(2) or (3) but the claimant is not content with the amount paid, the claimant may still start proceedings. However, the court will order the defendant to pay no more than the Stage 2 fixed costs where the court awards an interim payment of no more than the amount offered by the defendant or the court makes no award.'

This cost risk is repeated at CPR 45.24 (3)

> *'Where the claimant starts proceedings under paragraph 7.28 of the RTA Protocol or paragraph 7.26 of the EL/PL Protocol and the court orders the defendant to make an interim payment of no more than the interim payment made under paragraph 7.14(2) or (3) of the RTA Protocol or paragraph 7.17(2) or (3) of the EL/PL Protocol the court will, on the final determination of the proceedings, order the defendant to pay no more than –*
>
> *(a) the Stage 1 and 2 fixed costs; and*
>
> *(b) the disbursements allowed in accordance with rule 45.19.'*

The choice to withdraw a claim from the RTA Protocol should not be taken lightly and such decisions, based on an interim payment request, must be considered alongside the requirements of CPR r.25.7.

Exactly when procedurally an interim payment can be requested has been the subject of satellite litigation. Of particular contention is the interrelation between paragraph 7.12 (stay of proceedings) and 7.13

(request for an interim payment) and whether the need for both further expert evidence and a formal stay are required before interim payments can be requested.

The question was considered in *Luvin v Ageas Insuance Limited* (Birkenhead County Court, 17 September 2015) where DJ Doyle said the following about the interrelationship between 7.12 and 7.13;

> *'Just because these paragraphs have a separate heading, this does not imply any separate right to apply for an interim payment. There is no other paragraph within the protocol giving the right to an application for an interim payment to be made'*

In analysing the provisions within the RTA Protocol DJ Doyle concluded:

> *'If the claimant is content for their case to be disposed of on the current medical evidence, it will be dealt with quickly within the portal. In effect, the provisions of 7.70 provide for an interim payment to be made to them equal to the defendant's valuation of the claim, which will often be likely to be more than any interim payment they could expect under CPR r.25.7. However the claimant may wish to delay settlement for a number of reasons.......*
>
> *I am therefore satisfied that on any reading 7.12 must be a prerequisite of 7.13-17'*

If DJ Doyle's interpretation is correct a defendant should only face an application for an interim payment or the risk that a claim will be removed from the Portal under paragraph 7.29 where settlement is not yet possible because the evidence has not been finalised.

8. Defendant's Response

8.1. Timings (paragraph 7.35 – 7 37)

The case remains in Stage 2 for an initial period of 35 days after the Settlement Pack has been submitted to the defendant. The 'initial consideration period' of 15 days allows the defendant to consider the evidence provided and make an initial offer. The remaining time allows the parties to negotiate settlement and narrow the issues in dispute. The initial consideration period and the negotiation period can both be extended by consent. There is no maximum time limit on a claim progressing to Stage 3 and as such a claim could remain within Stage 2, with agreement of the parties for a significant period of time.

Where an offer is made by a party less than 5 days before the end of the total period (whether extended or not) the total period will automatically be extended by 5 days to allow a party to consider the offer made. During this automatic extension no further offers can be made and although not expressly mentioned it follows, due to the continuation of Stage 2, that Stage 3 proceedings cannot be commenced.

8.2. Evidence

In responding to a Stage 2 Settlement Pack submitted by the claimant the defendant has the following options:

(a) They can notify the claimant that they consider that the small claims track would be the normal track. This would result in the claim automatically falling from the RTA protocol and the matter would revert to being governed by the Pre-Action Protocol for Personal Injury Claims and the Practice Direction – Pre-Action Conduct and Protocols (paragraph 7.39(a));

(b) The admission of causation as defined in paragraph 1.1(1)(c) can be withdrawn. This again will result in the automatic withdrawal from the RTA Protocol. (paragraph 7.39(b);

(c) The claimant's valuation of the claim presented, or any individual head of loss can be agreed;

(d) A counter-offer, the heads of loss which remain in dispute, can be presented.

Where a head of loss is not agreed the defendant must propose alternative amount to facilitate the settlement of the head of loss. The defendant should also provide an explanation why a particular head of loss has not been agreed and the basis on which a counter-offer has been made. (Paragraph 7.41)

> '*When making a counter-offer the defendant must propose an amount for each head of damage and may, in addition, make an offer that is higher than the total of the amounts proposed for all heads of damage. The defendant must also explain in the counter-offer why a particular head of damage has been reduced. The explanation will assist the claimant when negotiating a settlement and will allow both parties to focus on those areas of the claim that remain in dispute.*'

There is no express provision within the RTA Protocol which allows a defendant to rely on any documentation, witness evidence or expert evidence. This is in stark contrast to the claimant, whose disclosure responsibilities and right to rely on evidence is clearly laid out in the express terms of the RTA Protocol. The only express provision for evidence and/or disclosure from the defendant are contained in paragraph 6.19A which allows the defendant to send an account of the accident circumstances when responding to the CNF and the disclosure of a certificate of recoverable benefits at Stage 1.

Paragraph 7.11 could arguably be interpreted to provide a defendant with an entitlement to serve witness evidence reasonably required to value the claim, but this is far from clear.

> *'In most cases, witness statements, whether from the claimant or otherwise, will not be, required. One or more statements may, however, be provided where reasonably required to value the claim.'*

It is potentially difficult to see how this sits with the judgment of HHJ Freedman in *Mulholland v Hughes* [2015] Lexis Citation 333 or the proclamation by LJ Jackson in *Phillips v Willis* [2016] EWCA Civ 401 that credit hire cases were suitable for consideration within the portal.

In *Mulholland v Hughes*, a case which also centred on a credit hire claim, the claimant pursued a claim for personal injury and the credit hire of an alternative vehicle. At Stage 2 the defendant disputed the hire claim and made a counter-offer of £1093.14. The reason provided by the defendant for the dispute was that they objected to the credit hire rate being applied. No other objections, such as duration or need, were raised by the defendant. Payment of the agreed amount was made but agreement for the outstanding amount could not be reached and the matter proceeded to a Stage 3 oral hearing. At this hearing DJ Kramer dismissed the claim for hire in its entirety on the basis that the claimant had failed to provide evidence of 'need' and ordered the repayment of the amount paid by the defendant towards the hire claim. Two other conjoined cases followed similar factual matrices and all three claimants appealed.

The appeals proceeded on three distinct issue, but it is the second of these '*if a defendant does not put a matter in issue at Stage 2, can the point still be taken at a Part 8 hearing before a judge?*' which is relevant to the discussion at hand.

In reversing the decision of the lower Courts HHJ Freedman stated at paragraph 75:

'It seems to me that what underpins these rules and practice directions is that it is incumbent upon a defendant to set out, with clarity, the precise nature of his defence: what is agreed, what is disputed and, if disputed, why, as well as indicating those matters upon which the defendant is unable to comment'

And at paragraph 77:

> *'It follows that it is the intention of the Protocol that if a defendant wishes to raise an issue such as the need for hire, that is to be done at the time of the making of the counter-offer. To allow a defendant to raise the issue of need at Stage 3 runs entirely contrary to the notion that at the end of Stage 2 the parties should have clarity as to what remains in dispute.'*

And at paragraph 80:

> *'In my judgment, it comes to this: to make an offer in respect of hire charges is not to admit the need for hire but not to challenge the need at Stage 2 is equivalent to saying that the claimant does not need formally to prove it. Such is the binding on the Court.'*

It is clear, therefore, that a defendant must highlight and explain the nature of their defence within Stage 2 and that a failure to do so will result in a defendant being debarred from relying on these arguments. The judgment does not, however, expressly provide guidance to what extent a defendant is allowed to rely on evidence. The judgment focuses primarily on the effect of an evidential and procedural ambush on the claimant's ability to evidence their case.

This apparent prohibition on a defendant relying on evidence is also inconsistent with paragraph 7.64(2)(a) which advocates that *'sup-*

porting comments and evidence from both parties on any disputed heads of damage' must be served before a claim may proceed further within the RTA Protocol.

In practical terms, the Courts have allowed defendants to upload and rely on documentary evidence to support their counter offers. This is rarely challenged as long as the documents are made available within Stage 2 and most courts are likely to apply a broad interpretation of paragraph 7.41.

9. Failure to reach agreement

If at the end of the total consideration period, the parties have not reached agreement on the amount of the damages payable the claimant must send the defendant a Court Proceedings Pack to mark the end of Stage 2. This requirement is triggered where agreement cannot be reached on the original damages or both the original and any additional damages.

The Court Proceedings Pack contains 2 distinct parts; A and B.

Part A of the Court Proceedings Pack reproduces the damages grid contained within the Stage 2 Settlement Pack and is supported by a statement of truth. The document requires the claimant to detail both parties' positions against each head of loss including the amount claimed, any contributory negligence deductions and any claim for interest.

Part B details the last offers made by both parties before the expiry of the consideration period and it is this document which is filed at Court in a sealed envelope pursuant to CPR PD8B para. 6.1(2). It is the differential between the Part B figure and the eventual judgment at Stage 3 which is compared for Part 36 purposes.

It is clear, given that the anonymity of Part B is maintained before the Court, that the Court envisages that a difference will exist between the figures at Part A (which is viewed by the Court) and Part B. This is also clear from the practitioners notes within Part B and the operation of Part 36.

The content of Part A should, therefore, be the original claim and counter-offer uploaded to the portal and the figures contained within Part B should be the final total figure after the parties have attempted reasonable negotiations.

If completed correctly the Part A and Part B figures should rarely be the same and the increased prospects of activating Part 36 sanctions should operate as a deterrent on both parties in proceeding to a Stage 3 hearing when the difference between the offers is minimal.

Any offers made by either parties after the total consideration period (including any agreed or automatic extensions) should not be included.

The defendant is under a duty to check the Court Proceedings Pack for compliance. Paragraph 7.67 states:

> *'The defendant should then check that the Court Proceedings Pack (Part A and Part B) Form complies with paragraphs 7.64 to 7.66. If the defendant considers that the Court Proceedings Pack (Part A and Part B) Form does not comply it must be returned to the claimant within 5 days with an explanation as to why it does not comply.'*

Although not expressly stated within the RTA Protocol, it appears implicit that a failure by a defendant to highlight non-compliance within 5 days would likely be seen as acceptance that the Pack was compliant. Such a failure would certainly provide a claimant with a valid objection if a defendant seeks to raise this issue at a stage 3 hearing.

Where settlement cannot be achieved a defendant must pay, within 15 days, the final offer made (i.e. the figure contained within Part B of the Court Proceedings Pack). Credit must be given for interim payments and deductible benefits (paragraph 7.70). Stage 1 and 2 fixed costs and allowable disbursements must also be paid by the defendant. Where agreement cannot be reached between the parties on the disbursements, the defendant must pay the disbursements which it considers were reasonably incurred (paragraph 7.71).

CHAPTER THREE
STAGE 3

1. Commencing Stage 3

Once the total consideration period has expired without settlement and the Court Proceedings Pack has been served Stage 2 comes to an end. The claimant must then make a request for the Court to determine damages by commencing proceedings pursuant to CPR Part 8. This is achieved by filing a claim form N208 which must include, pursuant to CPR PD8B para. 5.2, the following information:

'The claim form must state –

(1) that the claimant has followed the procedure set out in the relevant Protocol;

(2) the date when the Court Proceedings Pack (Part A and Part B) Form was sent to the defendant. (This provision does not apply where the claimant is a child and the application is for a settlement hearing);

(3) whether the claimant wants the claim to be determined by the court on the papers (except where a party is a child) or at a Stage 3 hearing;

(4) where the claimant seeks a settlement hearing or a Stage 3 hearing, the dates which the claimant requests should be avoided; and

(5) the value of the claim'

When commencing proceeding the claimant must also file, pursuant to CPR PD8B para. 6.1:

> *'(1) the Court Proceedings Pack (Part A) Form;*
>
> *(2) the Court Proceedings Pack (Part B) Form (the claimant and defendant's final offers) in a sealed envelope. (This provision does not apply where the claimant is a child and the application is for a settlement hearing);*
>
> *(3) copies of medical reports;*
>
> *(4) evidence of special damages; and*
>
> *(5) evidence of disbursements (for example the cost of any medical report) in accordance with rule 45.19(2).'*

A claimant is not entitled to rely on any evidence which is not included with the Claim Form and which has not previously been served on the defendant with the Court Proceedings Pack (CPR PD8B para 6.3 and 6.4).

Interestingly the provisions of CPR PD8 again appear to exclude the reliance of documentation by the defendant. Although CPR PD8B para. 7.1 makes reference to a parties' reliance on evidence it refers back to CPR PD8B para. 6.4, which exclusively allows a claimant to rely on documents if served in accordance with the Protocol. Other references to CPR PD8B para. 8.2 and 11.3 relate only to a defendant's acknowledgment of service and any certificate of recoverable benefits.

2. Defendant's response

As with all proceedings the defendant has 14 days within which to file and serve an acknowledgement of service. In acknowledging a

Part 8 claim a defendant has four options pursuant to CPR PD8 para.8.3. The defendant can confirm that they:

(a) contest the amount of damages claimed;

(b) contest the making of an order for damages;

(c) dispute the court's jurisdiction; or

(d) object to the use of the Stage 3 Procedure;

The practice directions expressly require the acknowledgement of service to be signed by the defendant's insurer (CPR r.8 PD 8.5). This directly contradicts CPR r.22.1 (6) which allows statements of truth on statements of case, a response or an application to be signed by a legal representative and reflects that fact that insurers in RTA claims are expected to take a central role in the settlement of liability admitted cases.

3. Consideration of the claim

Upon receipt of the Claim Form the Court will order that damages are assessed either on the papers or at an oral Stage 3 hearing (CPR PD8B para. 11.1). Either party may request that the matter is considered at an oral hearing or the Court may make such a determination on its own motion (CPR PD8B para 11.1(2)). Should an oral hearing be required, by either party, the parties will be given at least 21 days' notice of the hearing.

Where a claim is considered on the papers the Judgment must include the Courts reasoning for the quantum decision reached (CPR PD8 para. 11.4). Where judgment is determined on the papers it is not possible to apply for the judgment to be set aside and a formal appeal would be necessary (CPR PD8B para.15.1)

CHAPTER FOUR
ADMISSIONS AND SETTLEMENTS

1. Admissions

1.1. Scope and Definition

In admitting liability a defendant, pursuant to paragraph 1.1 (1) of the RTA Protocol, admits that

(a) the accident occurred;

(b) the accident was caused by the defendant's breach of duty;

(c) the defendant caused some loss to the claimant, the nature and extent of which is not admitted; and

(d) the defendant has no accrued defence to the claim under the Limitation Act 1980.

Once an admission has been made any argument which seeks to extinguish damages in their entirety should be unsuccessful.

In *Blake v Croasdale* [2017] EWCH 1336 (QB) a defence of *ex turpi causa,* relating to a road traffic accident which occurred whilst the claimant was selling drugs, was precluded by an admission of liability. Although the admission was not made via the correct procedure under the RTA Protocol and the claim later exited the portal His Honour Judge Purle QC (sitting as a Judge of the High Court) viewed the admission as being made within the portal and applied the definitions under paragraph 1.1(1).

The scope and definition of an RTA Protocol admission was not expressly considered in *Richards & Anor v Morris* [2018] EWHC 1289 (QB) when the claim was dismissed on appeal. Despite the existence of the admission being acknowledged it is not clear whether specific reliance was placed on the admission by the parties and no express ruling was made by Mr Justice Martin Spencer on the issue. Arguably fundamental dishonesty allegations are inconsistent to a protocol admission and should require an application to withdraw. It is a fair assumption, however, given the tone of the judgment, that a withdrawal would have been granted if requested.

In *Molodi v Cambridge Vibration Maintenance Services* it was made clear that arguments designed to extinguish individual heads of loss were not inconsistent with an admission of liability made at Stage 1. This conclusion was based on the existence of the caveat, contained within the definition of an admission at paragraph 1.1(d) of the RTA Protocol, that the nature and extent of damage is not admitted.

1.2. Force of admissions

In *Blake v Croasdale,* His Honour Judge Purle QC took the view that a protocol admission was binding and a formal application to withdraw was required if a defendant wished to avoid the claim.

The binding nature of a protocol admission was further explored in a series of cases where subsequent proceedings were issued in competition with an earlier admission.

In both *Ullah v Jon* (Croydon County Court 20 March 2013) and *Malak v Nasim* (Watford County Court, December 2014) the claimant's insurers settled claims pursued under the RTA Protocol on behalf of the defendant. The defendant drivers then issued their own separate personal injury claims. Disputes arose in these subsequent proceedings when the 'now defendants' placed reliance on the earlier insurer led admissions and applied for summary judgment on or strike out of the claims.

In both cases the binding nature of the admissions, within the confines of the individual claims in which the admissions were made, was accepted (although dispute existed in *Ullah v Jon* as to whether an insurer had authority to make such an admission). The Judgments, however, diverged when considering the wider implications of a Protocol admission on subsequent claims and which aspect of the CPR governed efforts to resile from the admission.

In *Ullah v Jon,* DJ Parker drew comparison between the RTA Protocol and the provisions of part 36. He took note of the prescriptive nature of both rules and concluded, as a consequence, that the admission was fully binding. In *Malak v Nasim*, DJ Wood took an opposing view and concluded that an admission was only binding in the claim in which it was made

Interestingly, DJ Parker and DJ Wood also took opposing views on which provision under CPR Part 14 applied. DJ Parker concluded that CPR 14.1A applied whereas DJ Wood concluded that CPR 14.1B applied.

This deadlock was address by HHJ Simpkiss in the appeal case of *Chimal v Chibwana & Williams* (Brighton CC, 27 October 2016) where an RTA Protocol admission was considered binding at first instance to *'avoid a multiplicity of proceedings, and the double jeopardy of conflicting decisions on the same facts'*. Although HHJ Simpkiss disagreed with DJ Hammond that double jeopardy existed (*in the strictest sense*) he mirrored the first instance conclusion and dismissed the appeal. In concluding that CPR 14.1B was the appropriate regime for withdrawal of the Protocol admission he stated:

> *'If an admission is made by a Portal Defendant that should be treated as any other admission, although on the facts of this case, it*

> *cannot now be withdrawn because the Portal claim was settled and there is no claim to which the Claimant in these proceedings is defendant'*

It is, therefore, clear that admissions made on protocol cases have wider application and are binding in subsequent cases.

2. Settlement

2.1. Status of Settlement

In *Fitton v Ageas*, a dispute arose between the parties as to whether an offer made by the claimant within the Protocol was open for acceptance and whether, once accepted, a claimant could rely on the doctorine of mistake to avoid the compromise reached. In allowing the defendant's appeal HHJ Parker stated:

> *'The offer had been made by the claimant, albeit mistakenly and the offer was accepted by the defendant, as the defendant was entitled so to do. Whether there was a meeting of minds between the parties or not did not matter. There was an offer within the Protocol made by the claimant and there was an acceptance within the Protocol made by the defendant. The matter was thereby compromised'*

In reaching this decision HHJ Parker considered that:

> *'there is very good reason for the Protocol to be self-contained, to the exclusion of normal principles of contact and, for example, the doctrine of mistake- because of the risk that the objective sought by the Protocol is thwarted by disproportionate satellite litigation.'*

2.2. Defendant's responsibilities

Following settlement of a claim (original damages and/or additional damages) the defendant must pay, within 10 days of settlement, the following (paragraph 7.44):

> *'(1) the Stage 1 and Stage 2 fixed costs in rule 45.18;*
>
> *(2) an agreement in principle to pay a sum equal to the Type C fixed costs of an additional advice on quantum of damages where such advice is justified under paragraph 7.10;*
>
> *(3) an agreement in principle to pay relevant disbursements allowed in accordance with rule 45.19;*
>
> *(3A) in a soft tissue injury claim, the cost of obtaining a medical report in rule 45.19(2A)(a);*
>
> *(4) where applicable, any success fee in accordance with rule 45.31(1) (as it was in force immediately before 1 April.'*

Pursuant to paragraph 7.47 credit must be given for any recoverable benefits, interim payments made and any fixed costs and disbursements already paid.

Attempts by a defendant to circumvent the RTA Protocol and avoid the responsibilities set out in paragraph 7.44 are unlikely to be successful. In *Gavin Edmonson Solicitors Ltd v Haven Insurance Ltd* [2018] UKSC 21 claims involving six different claimants were intimated under the RTA Protocol against defendants insured by Haven Insurance. Instead of responding within the portal settlement offers, excluding costs, were made directly to each claimant with a declaration that dealing directly would result in a more favourable and speedier settlement. All six claimants cancelled their CFAs and accepted the offers made. Gavin Edmonson Solicitors sued for recovery of their fixed costs. In rejecting the Defendant's appeal the Supreme Court concluded (paragraph 58):

> *'Furthermore the careful balance of competing interest enshrined in the RTA Protocol assumes that a solicitor's expectation of recovery of his charges from the Defendant's insurer is underpinned by the equitable lien, based as it is upon a sufficient responsibility of the client for those charges'*

2.3. Additional Claims

Vehicle related damages are initially expected to be dealt with outside the RTA Protocol. Despite this expectation it is clearly not the intent of the rules committee that vehicle related damage would ordinarily justify satellite litigation. This is confirmed by the string of judgments flowing from the issue of Part 7 proceedings following the in-portal settlement of related personal injury claims (*Smikle v Global Logistics, Reardon v Mango Engineering Services Ltd* and *Hillier v Southern Rock*) and HHJ Jackson's decision in *Phillips.*

Where the original damages have not settled during the consideration period the claimant must notify the defendant if additional damages, being pursued by a third party, remain outstanding and must amend the Stage 2 Settlement Pack to make an offer for these additional damages within the portal process (paragraph 7.52). A defendant upon receipt of the amended claim has 15 days to respond (paragraph 7.53). It is clear, therefore, that all disputed heads of loss are expected to proceed into Stage 3 on the same Claim Form.

Where the original damages have been settled but the additional damages remain live a claimant may issue Part 7 proceedings (paragraph 7.60(2)). It is notable that the deliberations in *Phillips v Willis* related to vehicle damage included within the original Settlement Pack but *Smikle v Global Logistics* and *Reardon v Mango Engineering*

Services Ltd both involved vehicle damage highlighted as being pursued by a third party. It unclear, therefore, where the issue of part 7 proceedings under paragraph 7.60(2) would be considered appropriate by the Court.

CHAPTER FIVE
COSTS

The RTA Protocol is the primary source of rules for governing behaviours in low value RTA claims and are supported and supplemented by sections of the CPR. This dynamic is no more demonstrated by the rules surrounding costs where the basic rights and behaviours controlling costs are set out within the RTA Protocol but are significantly supplemented by CPR r.45.15 to r.45.29.

Costs are an important and sometimes complex aspect of the RTA Protocol and the escalating costs of civil litigation was undoubtedly a guiding principle in establishing the Protocol in 2010. It is important to remember that payment of costs to the claimant's legal representative at each appropriate stage is a primary aim of the RTA Protocol (paragraph 1.1(3)).

Consistent with this desire to limit the expense of litigation, costs are limited to the categories as set out in CPR r.45.17:

> *'The only costs allowed are –*
>
> *(a) fixed costs in rule 45.18; and*
>
> *(b) disbursements in accordance with rule 45.19; and*
>
> *(c) where applicable, fixed costs in accordance with rule 45.23A or 45.23B.'*

1. Fixed costs

The amount of costs is then strictly controlled by Table 6 under CPR r.45.18.

Fixed costs in relation to the RTA Protocol			
Where the value of the claim for damages is not more than £10,000		**Where the value of the claim for damages is more than £10,000, but not more than £25,000**	
Stage 1 fixed costs	£200	Stage 1 fixed costs	£200
Stage 2 fixed costs	£300	Stage 2 fixed costs	£600
Stage 3 – Type A fixed costs	£250	Stage 3 – Type A fixed costs	£2500
Stage 3 –Type B Fixed costs	£250	Stage 3 –Type B fixed costs	£250
Stage 3 – Type C fixed costs	£150	Stage 3 – Type C fixed Costs	£150

Pursuant to CPR r.45.18 (5) a 12.5% uplift in the costs at all stages is applicable where the claimant lives and the solicitor instructed practices in areas *'served by the County Court hearing centres at Barnet, Brentford, Central London, Clerkenwell and Shoreditch, Edmonton, Ilford, Mayors and City of London, Romford, Wandsworth and Willesden and (outside London) the County Court hearing centres at Bromley, Croydon, Dartford, Gravesend and Uxbridge'* (CPR PD 45 para. 2.6). It is important to note that eligibility for the uplift requires both the claimant and their solicitor to be based within the identified locations.

VAT is also recoverable, where appropriate, on the figures quoted in CPR r.45.18.

2. Disbursements

Disbursements are also restricted by CPR r.45.19 and a Court will not award disbursements which are not detailed in CPR r.45.19 (2) and r.45.19 (3). The following costs are expressly recoverable from the defendant:

1. Medical records (45.19(2)(a)(i));
2. DVLA search (45.19(2)(aa));
3. Motor Insurance Database search (45.19(2)(bb);
4. Court fees where protective proceedings are issued (45.19(2)(c));
5. Court fees linked to the issue of Part 8 proceedings for Stage 3 (45.19(2)(d);
6. Court fees linked to the need for infant approval pursuant to CPR r.21 (45.19(2)(b);
7. The costs in connections with the instruction of a medical expert(s) (45.19(2)(a)(ii));
8. The costs in connections with the instruction of a non-medical expert(s) allowable within the Protocol (45.19(2)(a)(ii));
9. The fee for an engineer's report; (45.19(2)(a)(i)).

The total amount claimable for each disbursement category is not defined, save for disbursements relating to medical expert reports. The cost related concepts of reasonableness and proportionality will still apply to any claim for reimbursement. In respect to medical related disbursement CPR r.45.19 2A applies such that most medical related disbursements are limited to the following designated fixed fees:

'(2A) *In a soft tissue injury claim to which the RTA Protocol applies, the only sums (exclusive of VAT) that are recoverable in respect of the cost of obtaining a fixed cost medical report or medical records are as follows—*

(a) obtaining the first report from an accredited medical expert selected via the MedCo Portal: £180;

(b) obtaining a further report where justified from an expert from one of the following disciplines—

(i) Consultant Orthopaedic Surgeon (inclusive of a review of medical records where applicable): £420;

(ii) Consultant in Accident and Emergency Medicine: £360;

(iii) General Practitioner registered with the General Medical Council: £180; or

(iv) Physiotherapist registered with the Health and Care Professions Council: £180;

(c) obtaining medical records: no more than £30 plus the direct cost from the holder of the records, and limited to £80 in total for each set of records required. Where relevant records are required from more than one holder of records, the fixed fee applies to each set of records required;

(d) addendum report on medical records (except by Consultant Orthopaedic Surgeon): £50; and

(e) answer to questions under Part 35: £80.'

CPR r.45.19 (2) (e) provides that '*any other disbursement reasonably incurred due to a particular feature of the dispute*' will also be recoverable. Despite the apparent open-ended nature of this provision until recently there was surprisingly little case law is available to assist in interpreting its scope and no binding precedents. Two competing first instance decisions were available.

In *Madej v Maciszyn* [2013] Lexis Citation 143 the court considered the application of CPR r.45.12 (2) (c), an identically worded provision for cases which pre-date the RTA Protocol. The claimant, a Polish national, was injured in a road traffic accident in January 2010. Settlement was achieved without the need for proceedings based on medical evidence obtained with the assistance of a Polish interpreter. Agreement on costs could not be achieved and 'cost only' proceedings were issued and heard by Master Campbell, sitting in the High Court as a cost judge. Master Cambell concluded that CPR r.45.12 (2) (c) was a sweep up provision and that the costs were necessary to progress the claim presented.

In *Olesiej v Maple Industries* (Liverpool County Court, 4 Janauary 2012) HHJ Graham Wood QC disallowed the translator's fees incurred on almost identical grounds. Applying a very narrow interpretation of the phrase '*due to a particular feature of the dispute*', Judge Wood concluded that the inability to speak English was a characteristic of the claimant and not of the dispute.

The recent case of *Aldred v Cham* [2019] EWCA Civ 1780, however, saw the Court of Appeal addressing these inconsistencies and providing useful guidance on the recoverability of disbursements in fixed fee RTA cases. It is unlikely, however, that the judgment of Lord Justice McCombe, Lord Justice Coulson and Lady Justice Davies will be the end of this matter with an appeal to the Supreme Court anticipated.

Although the case related to fixed costs under CPR r.45 IIIA, where the claim has exited the RTA Protocol, the wording of the catch all provisions in CPR r.45 III and CPR r.45 IIIA is identical. The judgment is, therefore, highly likely to be binding on claims which proceed within the portal.

In *Aldred v Cham*, a claim for recovery of Counsel's fee incurred for a quantum advice obtained in compliance with CPR r.21 was rejected by the defendant. The claim proceeded to both paper and oral cost hearings before District Judge Hale where recovery of the disbursement was allowed. The matter was appealed which HHJ Owen QC allowed and commented as follows:

> *'If the claimant is a child, the need to obtain counsel's advice on valuation would constitute a particular feature of the dispute. There is no justification for implying that those fees, when incurred, are already provided for within the fixed recoverable costs'*

A further appeal was submitted.

In allowing the appeal and rejecting recovery of counsel's fee, Coulson LJ considered the parameters of CPR r.45.29I (2) (h) and asked two distinct questions:

(a) was counsel's advice 'due to a particular feature of the dispute' pursuant to CPR r.45.29I(2)(h)

(b) if the advice was due to a particular feature of the dispute, was the cost thereof a disbursement reasonably incurred which the court should allow, in addition to the fixed recoverable costs?

In considering the first of these issues, LJ Coulson applied a very narrow interpretation to the phrase '*a feature of the dispute*' noting at paragraph 35:

> *'The fact that, in a particular case, a claimant is a child, or someone who cannot speak English, or who requires an interme-*

diary, is nothing whatever to do with the dispute itself. Age, linguistic ability and mental wellbeing are all characteristics of the claimant regardless of the dispute. They are not generated by or linked in any way to the dispute itself and cannot therefore be said to be a particular feature of that dispute.'

He continues by providing guidance on the types of issues which he considered could potentially give rise to a recoverable cost under CPR r.45.29I (2) (h). These, highlighted as being fact specific, include disputes concerning the mechanism of the accident, liability and the nature of the injuries sustained.

The judgment acknowledged the two competing first instance cases of *Olesiej v Maple Industries* and *Madej v Maciszyn* but in preferring *Olesiej*, LJ Coulson applied HHJ Wood's rationale to the recoverability of disbursements required for child claimants.

In practical terms, once the Court of Appeal concluded that the instruction of Counsel fell outside the definition of CPR 45.29I (2) (h) there was no requirement to consider the reasonableness of the costs incurred. LJ Coulson, however, concluded that the relevant activity (i.e. a quantum assessment by Counsel) was an ordinary litigation activity which was intrinsically covered within the fixed cost regime allowable under CPR 45.29C.

As matters stand, therefore, the definition of '*due to a particular feature of the dispute*' is to be interpreted narrowly and is unlikely to cover any costs incurred due to a characteristic of a particular claimant;

Although the amounts in dispute are relatively small this ruling could have wide reaching implications for claimants and their representatives. There are concerns that it will disproportionately affect certain aspects of society who, by their very nature, may incur costs which are not ordinarily part of litigation. In particular, children, non-English speakers and those with disabilities (e.g. deafness) are likely to have higher than average disbursement deductions from the standard fixed fee and as such there may be significant reductions in the fee received for representing these individuals.

There is no evidence, within the judgment, that the Lord Justices were expressly asked to consider these issues relating to access to justice, human rights or potential discrimination. Reference was, however, made to the gains and losses experienced overall in a fixed cost regime as set out in *Sharpe v Leeds City Council* [2017] 4 WLR 98 suggesting that the Lord Justices accepted that some comparative inconsistencies were justifiable.

Some comparison can be drawn between this issue and the Unison challenge of employment tribunal fees, although clear statistical evidence was available to show the detrimental effect of the fee regime on claim numbers in that case.

An appeal to the Supreme Court is anticipated and it will, undoubtedly, be this aspect which attracts future litigation and, will in all likelihood, become a central issue in any appeal to the Supreme Court.

3. CPR Part 36

3.1. General Provisions

CPR 36 II applies to compliant offers made where the RTA Protocol has been followed and Part 8 proceedings have been issued. A party is entitled to make an offer in whichever format they chose but non-compliant offers may not attract cost consequences (CPR r.36.24 (4))

A compliant protocol offer must be included within Part B of the Court Proceedings Pack (CPR r.36.25 (2) (a)) and is inclusive of interest (CPR r.36.27 (a)). Compliant protocol offers must not be communicated to the Court until judgment has been entered and the sealed envelope is opened when costs are considered.

3.2. Cost Consequences

The primary aim of the RTA Protocol, to achieve quick settlement and avoid spiralling costs, is closely linked with the clear desire to encourage parties to negotiate settlement and to actively consider reasonable efforts made to settle the claim. These expectations are enshrined in the provisions of CPR r.36.29 which set out the cost consequences on parties who fail to consider reasonable offers.

Where a claimant achieves a judgment which is more than the defendant's offer but less than the claimant's offer the status quo is maintained and ordinary fixed costs under CPR r.45.20 apply.

Where the claimant fails to beat the defendant's portal offer the claimant will be ordered to pay the defendant's costs pursuant to CPR r.45.26:

> *'Where rule 36.29(1) (a) applies, the court will order the claimant to pay –*
>
> *(a) where the claim is determined –*
>
> *(i) on the papers, Stage 3 Type A fixed costs; or*
>
> *(ii) at a hearing, Stage 3 Type A and B fixed costs;*
>
> *(b) any Stage 3 disbursements allowed in accordance with rule 45.19'*

The defendant retains a duty to pay stage 1 and 2 fixed costs and disbursements which should have been paid at the end of each relevant stage.

Where the claimant receives a judgment which equal to or exceeds their Part B offer the cost sanctions contained in CPR r.36.29 (4). Additional payment must be made by the defendant in the following terms:

> *'the court must order the defendant to pay—*
>
> *(a) interest on the whole of the damages awarded at a rate not exceeding 10% above base rate for some or all of the period starting with the date specified in rule 36.26;*
>
> *(b) the fixed costs in rule 45.20;*
>
> *(c) interest on those fixed costs at a rate not exceeding 10% above base rate; and*
>
> *(d) an additional amount calculated in accordance with rule 36.17(4) (d).'*

The date for the calculation of interest on damages is defined by CPR r.36.26 as the first business day after the receipt of the Settlement Pack. Rather oddly, there is no defined date for the calculation of interest on costs within the RTA Protocol. It is likely that most Judges will utilise the period defined in CPR r.36.26 although parties should be prepared to make or deal with arguments that interest on costs should be calculated over a shorter period of time.

The rate of interest is open to the Court's discretion. It should be remembered that the provision in CPR r.36.29 are punitive in nature and whilst an award at the very top end of the scale is unlikely in the current financial environment, an interest award could be significantly increase both costs and damages.

CHAPTER SIX
WITHDRAWAL

The RTA Protocol is designed for cases which have limited areas of dispute and complexity. There are, therefore, numerous points where cases automatically fall from the process or where a party may actively choose to remove a case.

1. Routes to withdrawal

1.1. Further evidence required

Once Part 8 proceedings have been issued the parties may not rely on any evidence which has not been filed and served (CPR PD 8B para.7.1). Pursuant to CPR PD 8B para.7.2

> *'Where the court considers that –*
>
> *(1) further evidence must be provided by any party; and*
>
> *(2) the claim is not suitable to continue under the Stage 3 Procedure,*
>
> *the court will order that the claim will continue under Part 7, allocate the claim to a track and give directions.'*

This is to be contrasted with the Court's case management duties preserved within CPR PD 8B para.7.1 (3) which allows a Court to order disclosure of further evidence *'where the court considers that it cannot properly determine the claim without it'*. It would appear that the determining factor in the operation of CPR PD8B para.7.1 (3) and CPR PD8B para.7.2 is a determination of the suitability of Stage 3 of the RTA Protocol.

In *Philips v Willis*, LJ Jackson held back no punches in his assessment that a case management decision to remove a case from the RTA Protocol for want of evidence was '*irrational*'. In his *obiter dicta* LJ Jackson expressed his opinion that the operation of CPR PD 8B para.7.2 was reserved for complex disputes.

1.2. Defendant opposes the claim

Pursuant to CPR PD 8B para.9.1 a Court will dismiss a claim commenced under CPR Part 8 were a defendant opposes the claim because a claimant has not followed the RTA Protocol procedure or the claimant filed and served additional evidence which had not been provided at Stage 2. The claimant can commence new proceedings under CPR Part 7 but will face any relevant arguments under the Limitation Act 1980 and CPR 45.24.

1.3. Withdrawal of an offer

There is no provision within the RTA Protocol which allows the withdrawal of an offer made at Stage 2 before the expiry of the total consideration period. Withdrawal of any parties offer after the consideration period but before the issue of proceedings will automatically cause the claim to fall from the portal pursuant to paragraph 7.46:

> *'Where a party withdraws an offer made in the Stage 2 Settlement Pack Form after the total consideration period or further consideration period, the claim will no longer continue under this Protocol and the claimant may start proceedings under Part 7 of the CPR'*

After proceedings have been issued an offer can only be withdrawn with the Court's permission pursuant to CPR PD 8B para.10.1:

'A party may only withdraw a Protocol offer after proceedings have been started with the court's permission. Where the Court gives permission the claim will no longer continue under the Stage 3 Procedure and the court will give directions. The court will only give permission where there is good reason for the claim not to continue under the Stage 3 Procedure'

1.4. General Case Management Discretion

The Court arguably retains the pervasive case management discretion to transfer a case to Part 7 pursuant to CPR 8 r.8.3:

'The Court may at any stage order the claim to continue as if the claimant had not used the Part 8 procedure and, if it does so, the court may give any directions it considers appropriate'

CPR PD 8B para. 2.2 does not expressly exclude the Court's general case management discretion, although it is notable that other commentators suggest that the power, under CPR PD para. 8.3, is not available to the Court in cases being pursued under the RTA Protocol. LJ Jackson at paragraph 37 of his judgment in *Philips v Willis* confirms that CPR r 8.1(3) can apply but with reservations:

'I am bound to accept that the language of r 8.1(3) is wider than the language of para 7.2 of the practice direction. On the other hand, CPR 8.1(3) cannot be used to subvert the protocol process'

1.5. Value

A claim will fall from the Portal where it becomes clear that the value of the claim sits outside the lower and upper limits. It is incumbent on the claimant to assess the value of the claim and notify the defendant if a claim value exceeds the upper limit pursuant to paragraph 4.3:

> '*This Protocol ceases to apply to a claim where, at any stage, the claimant notifies the defendant that the claim has now been revalued at more than the Protocol upper limit.*"

It is clearly envisaged that the Defendant will be the party who takes a view on the lower value of the claim as set out in paragraph 6.15 4(b). If, however, a claimant is shown not to have held a reasonable belief of a claims value or delayed in notifying a defendant that the value has changed a court may apply sanctions.

In *Cable v Liverpool Victoria Insurance* [2017] EWCA Civ 366 a high-income earner suffered neurological problems following a road traffic accident. It was originally intimated via the RTA Protocol in 2014 on the basis of a soft tissue injury without requiring any absence from work. In 2015 a neurological report was commissioned which confirmed that the claimant had in fact been absent from work since the accident. The claimant, unfortunately, failed to reassess the value of the claim at this stage. In 2017 Part 8 proceedings were issued and a stay obtained under paragraph 5.7. It was not until 2018 that the claims potential value was communicated and the transfer to Part 7 was sought. The claim was struck out as an abuse of process, a judgment upheld on appeal by HHJ Wood, on the basis that the claimant did not hold a reasonable belief that the value was below the upper level.

1.6. Withdrawal of the admission on causation

Once the initial consideration period has expired a Defendant can withdraw their admission of causation that '*the defendant caused some loss to the claimant*'. Where notice is given of this withdrawal the claim will no longer continue under the Protocol pursuant to paragraph 7.39.

If the Defendant wishes to withdraw the admission of liability the procedure under CPR 14.1B would need to be followed and the claim would necessarily fall from the portal.

1.7. Voluntary removal

At various stages, where a defendant has breached the RTA Protocol procedure or the Protocol is considered unsuitable, a claim may be removed from the portal with notification from the claimant. It is important to note that written notification is usually required.

Paragraph 6.19 – '*Where the defendant fails to pay the Stage 1 fixed recoverable costs within the period specified in paragraph 6.18 the claimant may give written notice that the claim will no longer continue under this Protocol. Unless the claimant's notice is sent to the defendant within 10 days after the expiry of the period in paragraph 6.18 the claim will continue under this Protocol.*'

Paragraph 7.75 – Where the defendant does not comply with paragraphs 7.72 or 7.74 the claimant may give written notice that the claim will no longer continue under this Protocol and start proceedings under Part 7 of the CPR.

Paragraph 7.76 – Where the claimant gives notice to the defendant that the claim is unsuitable for this Protocol (for example, because there are complex issues of fact or law) then the claim will no longer continue under this Protocol.

2. Consequences of withdrawal

It is clear that the Courts have an expectation that where a case meets the basic criteria set out in paragraph 4.1 that the case will remain in the RTA Protocol process and that removal should be the exception and not the norm. This is made clear at paragraph 11 of LJ Jackson's judgment in *Phillips v Willis*:

> *'It is important to note that the RTA process has an inexorable character. If a case falls within the parameters of the RTA process, the parties must take the designated steps or accept the consequences. The rules specify what those consequences are. The rules also specify when a case must remain in the RTA process, when it must drop out of the process, and when it may drop out of the process.'*

Simple breaches of the rules do not automatically justify the removal of a case from the RTA Protocol and the unjustified removal of a case will expose a claimant to cost risks when separate proceedings are commenced under CPR Part 7. It is notable that there are no express cost consequences on a Defendant who needlessly removes a case from the RTA Protocol. This can probably be explained by the fact that a Claimant would be entitled to the enhanced fixed costs allowable under 45 IIIA in any event.

A claimant's costs recovery will be limited to the basic protocol fixed costs allowed under CPR r.45.18 where the Court considers that the removal was unjustified and/or caused by the Claimant's conduct. CPR r.45.24 confirms:

> *'(2) Subject to paragraph (2A), where a judgment is given in favour of the claimant but –*
>
> > *(a) the court determines that the defendant did not proceed with the process set out in the relevant Protocol because*

the claimant provided insufficient information on the Claim Notification Form;

(b) the court considers that the claimant acted unreasonably –

(i) by discontinuing the process set out in the relevant Protocol and starting proceedings under Part 7;

(ii) by valuing the claim at more than £25,000, so that the claimant did not need to comply with the relevant Protocol; or

(iii) except for paragraph (2)(a), in any other way that caused the process in the relevant Protocol to be discontinued; or

(c) the claimant did not comply with the relevant Protocol at all despite the claim falling within the scope of the relevant Protocol,

the court may order the defendant to pay no more than the fixed costs in rule 45.18 together with the disbursements allowed in accordance with rule 45.19'

The operation of CPR 45.24, to curtail a claimant's right to recover costs over and above protocol fixed costs, requires a determination that the decision to withdraw the claim was unreasonable. The assessment of unreasonable conduct suggests a range of behaviours and requires the Court to exercise its discretion. A variety of case law exists which is informative to predict the Court's approach to the assessment of unjustified removal. Given, however, that such decisions are fact specific they are unlikely to provide an exhaustive list of instances where costs will be limited as a consequence of unjust removal.

3. Case analysis

In Javkishan Patel v Fortis Insurance Ltd a claim was commenced via the RTA Protocol and 2 days later the Insurer responded in compliance with paragraph 6.11. The claimant withdrew the case from the Portal on the basis that no electronic acknowledgment had be provided in breach of paragraph 6.10. Proceedings were issued pursuant to CPR Part 7. In limiting the claimant's costs to RTA Protocol fixed costs Mr Recorder Morgan concluded that a breach of paragraph 6.10 did not give the Claimant the right to discontinue the Protocol.

In *Coggon v Irvine* (County Court at Birkenhead, 17 October 2014) the failure of a defendant to pay damages and costs within 10 days of settlement, in breach of the mandatory provisions of paragraphs 7.47 and 7.44, was considered unreasonable. In limiting costs to fixed portal costs the Court were persuaded by the lack of express sanction within the RTA Protocol and the clear difference drawn between a failure to pay an interim payment and final payments within the wording of the Protocol.

In *Modhwadia v Modhwadia* (Leicester County Court, 20 January 2015) the claim was commenced within the portal and liability was admitted. The matter proceeded into Stage 2 of the RTA Protocol process with the Settlement Pack being uploaded to the portal on 31 May 2012. In response the Defendant made a counter-offer but failed to provide an explanation in breach of the mandatory requirements set out at paragraph 7.41. After a brief period of negotiation the claimant commenced proceedings under CPR Part 7 on the basis that the failure to explain the counter offer effectively voided the offer and triggered an automatic withdrawal under paragraph 7.40. In dismissing the claimant's appeal HHJ Hampton rejected the submission that an automatic trigger had been activated and concluded that lack of explanation was not fundamental to the operation of the RTA Protocol on the facts of the case.

A failure to enter negotiations beyond the initial offer was also considered insufficient to justify the removal of a case from the RTA Protocol in *Ilahi v Usman* (Manchester County Court 20 November 2012). HHJ Platts also determined that the claimant's withdrawal of a portal offer to deliberately manipulate cost provisions was itself unreasonable behaviour which warranted the restriction of costs.

The Court's discretion to limit cost recovery under CPR r.45.21 is not limited to the voluntary withdrawal of cases from the RTA Protocol. The Court has shown a willingness to curtail cost recovery where the automatic exit of cases can be directly linked to a claimant's conduct.

In *Doyle v Manchester Audi* the application of CPR 45.36 (the predecessor provision to 45.24) was tested when a claim automatically exited the Portal at stage 1 following an alleged failure of the defendant to respond in breach of paragraph 6.11. In limiting the claimant's costs the Court concluded that the exit, despite the automatic nature of the trigger, was caused as a direct result of their failure to provide necessary information, namely the claimant's identity and address, and that this failure was sufficient to active the costs sanctions.

Similarly, in *Hussain v Wardle* (Stoke on Trent County Court, 25 February 2017) the claimant's failure to complete mandatory fields within the CNF was sufficient to activate CPR r.45.24 cost consequences despite the fact that the decision to remove the claim was taken by the defendant in line with the provisions of paragraph 6.8(1).

The application of CPR r. 45.24 to cases settled by way of a Part 36 offer before judgment was considered by DDJ Corscadden in

Rafiana v All Type Scaffolding Ltd (Manchester County Court, 14 January 2015). The claimant commenced Part 7 proceedings following their voluntary removal of the case from the RTA Protocol on the basis that the Defendant had failed to enter reasonable negotiations. The matter settled via Part 36 and proceeded to detailed assessment in order to consider whether the claimant's entitlement to cost should be limited under CPR r. 45.24. The wording of CPR r.45.24 (2) was considered as a preliminary issue with DDJ Corscadden confirming:

> *'In my judgment, there is clearly a settlement here. It would be wrong, in my Judgment, to construe that C.P.R. 45.24(2) should not apply because I consider the word "judgment" extends to include a settlement of the sort reached here. There was a deemed order here as per C.P.R. 44.9'*

This analysis supported previous similar first instance judgments in *Coggon v Irvine* and *Davies v Greenway LTL 19/11/2013.*

In *Brown v Ezeugwa* (Tunbridge Wells County Court, 12 January 2014) the wording of a settlement agreement was interrogated with the claimant arguing that an agreement to pay costs on a standard basis precluded the restriction of costs by CPR r.45.36 (now CPR45.24). In allowing the appeal HHJ Simpkiss concluded that assessing costs on a 'standard basis' included the courts discretion to restrict costs under CPR r.45.36.

Caution must also be exercised in retrospectively identifying a reason for withdrawal or trying to justify withdrawal with a factual situation which developed after the case dropped from the Portal.

In *Tennant v Cottrell* (Liverpool CC 11 December 2014) the claim fell from the RTA Protocol due to a zero offer being made against a single head of loss. The matter, however, then proceeded to fully contested Part 7 proceedings. In limiting costs DJ Jenkinson stated:

'In my judgment, it is necessary to look at whether or not the claimant's solicitors acted reasonably in giving that notice at the time that they brought the matter out of the portal, rather than imputing hindsight'

'A Practical Guide to Spousal Maintenance' by Liz Cowell
'A Practical Guide to the Law of Domain Names and Cybersquatting' by Andrew Clemson
'A Practical Guide to the Law of Gender Pay Gap Reporting' by Harini Iyengar
'A Practical Guide to the Rights of Grandparents in Children Proceedings' by Stuart Barlow
'NHS Whistleblowing and the Law' by Joseph England
'Employment Law and the Gig Economy' by Nigel Mackay & Annie Powell
'A Practical Guide to the General Data Protection Regulation (GDPR)' by Keith Markham
'A Practical Guide to Noise Induced Hearing Loss (NIHL) Claims' by Andrew Mckie, Ian Skeate, Gareth McAloon
'An Introduction to Beauty Negligence Claims – A Practical Guide for the Personal Injury Practitioner' by Greg Almond
'Intercompany Agreements for Transfer Pricing Compliance' by Paul Sutton
'Zen and the Art of Mediation' by Martin Plowman
'A Practical Guide to the SRA Principles, Individual and Law Firm Codes of Conduct 2019 – What Every Law Firm Needs to Know' by Paul Bennett
'A Practical Guide to Licensing Law for Commercial Property Lawyers' by Niall McCann & Richard Williams
'A Practical Guide to Adoption for Family Lawyers' by Graham Pegg
'A Practical Guide to Industrial Disease Claims' by Andrew Mckie & Ian Skeate
'A Practical Guide to Redundancy' by Philip Hyland
'A Practical Guide to Vicarious Liability' by Mariel Irvine
'A Practical Guide to Claims Arising from Delays in Diagnosing Cancer' by Bella Webb
'A Practical Guide to Applications for Landlord's Consent and Variation of Leases' by Mark Shelton
'A Practical Guide to Relief from Sanctions Post-Mitchell and Denton' by Peter Causton
'A Practical Guide to Equity Release for Advisors' by Paul Sams
'A Practical Guide to Unlawful Eviction and Harassment' by Stephanie Lovegrove

‘A Practical Guide to the Law Relating to Food’ by Ian Thomas
‘A Practical Guide to the Ending of Assured Shorthold Tenancies’ by Elizabeth Dwomoh
‘A Practical Guide to Financial Services Claims’ by Chris Hegarty
‘The Law of Houses in Multiple Occupation: A Practical Guide to HMO Proceedings’ by Julian Hunt
‘A Practical Guide to Unlawful Eviction and Harassment’ by Stephanie Lovegrove
‘A Practical Guide to Solicitor and Client Costs’ by Robin Dunne
‘A Practical Guide to Wrongful Conception, Wrongful Birth and Wrongful Life Claims’ by Rebecca Greenstreet
‘Occupiers, Highways and Defective Premises Claims: A Practical Guide Post-Jackson – 2nd Edition’ by Andrew Mckie
‘A Practical Guide to Financial Ombudsman Service Claims’ by Adam Temple & Robert Scrivenor
‘A Practical Guide to the Law of Enfranchisement and Lease Extension’ by Paul Sams
‘A Practical Guide to Marketing for Lawyers – 2nd Edition’ by Catherine Bailey & Jennet Ingram
'A Practical Guide to Advising Schools on Employment Law' by Jonathan Holden
'Certificates of Lawful Use and Development: A Guide to Making and Determining Applications' by Bob Mc Geady & Meyric Lewis
‘A Guide to Consent in Clinical Negligence Post-Montgomery’ by Lauren Sutherland QC
‘A Practical Guide to Running Housing Disrepair and Cavity Wall Claims: 2nd Edition’ by Andrew Mckie & Ian Skeate
‘A Practical Guide to Holiday Sickness Claims – 2nd Edition’ by Andrew Mckie & Ian Skeate
‘Arguments and Tactics for Personal Injury and Clinical Negligence Claims’ by Dorian Williams
‘A Practical Guide to QOCS and Fundamental Dishonesty’ by James Bentley
‘A Practical Guide to Drone Law’ by Rufus Ballaster, Andrew Firman, Eleanor Clot
‘A Practical Guide to Compliance for Personal Injury Firms Working With Claims Management Companies’ by Paul Bennett

www.ingramcontent.com/pod-product-compliance
Lightning Source LLC
LaVergne TN
LVHW022309200926
848481LV00004B/1257
9781912687619